RED EARTH

R ED EARTH

■ *Poems of New Mexico*

BY ALICE CORBIN

Compiled and edited by
Lois Rudnick and
Ellen Zieselman

MUSEUM OF
NEW MEXICO PRESS
SANTA FE

Project editor: Mary Wachs
Design and production: David Skolkin
Manufactured in China
10 9 8 7 6 5 4 3 2 1

ISBN: 0-89013-450-2 (CB)

Museum of New Mexico Press
Post Office Box 2087
Santa Fe, New Mexico 87504

PAGE ii

REBECCA SALSBURY JAMES

Earth and Water, 1950
Reverse oil on glass, 19 3/4 × 16 in.
Museum of New Mexico, Museum of Fine Arts
Bequest of Helen Miller Jones, 1986

CONTENTS

PREFACE
By Ellen Zieselman,
Curator of Education, Museum of Fine Arts

"PRETENTIOUS AS IT SOUNDS," wrote Tony Hillerman, "and tough as it is to prove, there *does* seem to be something about New Mexico which not only attracts creative people but stimulates their creativity" (vii).

A perusal of early numbers of *El Palacio*, the magazine of the Museum of New Mexico, reveals a balance of institutional interests ranging from archaeology to visual arts to literature that very well summarizes the kind of town that Alice Corbin and William Penhallow Henderson found themselves in when tuberculosis called Alice, along with so many others, to the desert.

In 1909, the Territorial Legislature of New Mexico chartered the Museum of New Mexico, inaugurated the following year in the historic Palace of the Governors on the downtown plaza. Though primarily an archaeological and history museum—indeed, it was founded as a coventure between the School of American Archaeology and the Historical Society of New Mexico—Taos and Santa Fe artists, whose art-colony towns did not yet provide galleries, were exhibiting their work in the Palace by 1915, and by 1917 numerous artists, including William Penhallow Henderson, were working out of studios provided there. The demands of a burgeoning art community led Museum of New Mexico Director Edgar L. Hewett to undertake the construction of an Art Gallery, today known as the Museum of Fine Arts, which opened in November of 1917.

New York artist Robert Henri had visited Santa Fe and advised Hewett that the new Museum of Fine Arts should have an open-door policy regarding exhibitions and showcase art being created in New Mexico. Taking his advice, Hewett created the first contemporary art museum in the United States and a wonderfully egalitarian exhibition space. Legend has it that exhibitions evolved from a pad of paper placed in the museum lobby, on which any artist could add his or her name. In time, as one's name reached the top of the list, the artist was given an alcove in which to create, exhibit, or sell artworks. Hewett reflected on the open-door policy in 1937: "Its alcoves have been open to the most eminent painter or sculptor, to the unknown beginner . . . all on equal terms. There has been no jury, no favoritism for any theory, or 'school' of art. . . . We believe firmly in the integration of the arts, of all the agencies that bring beauty and harmony into the lives of men" (Robertson and Nestor 150).

No environment could have been more propitious for the poet Alice Corbin Henderson and her artist-husband.

Santa Fe in the nineteen teens and twenties was home to a close-knit, supportive, and often raucous arts community. "Visiting, talking, partying are essential recreations for artists," observed Ruth Laughlin in 1949. "Evenings at the [John and Dolly] Sloans', the [Alice and William] Hendersons', Hal Bynner's, or Mary Austin's offered exchange of thoughts and often heated arguments" (Weigle and Fiore, 120). Poets, painters, sculptors, printmakers, novelists, musicians, dancers, and actors all lived as neighbors and friends. Artists formed alliances in order to sell or exhibit their artwork, poets pooled their limited resources in order to publish, and the Museum of Fine Arts proudly played host to both.

The poetry community was closely allied with the artists of the colony, perhaps because the chief poet in residence, Alice Corbin, was married to one of its more acclaimed artists, William Penhallow Henderson. Together, Alice and William helped to shape the Santa Fe art colony. A group of poets met regularly at the Henderson house on Camino del Monte Sol. Spud Johnson claimed they "seemed to lapse so often into a Rabelasian mood that soon we were referring to ourselves as the Rabelais Club, which was quickly altered, since that sounded much too stodgy, to the simple informality of 'The Rabble'" (Weigle and Fiore 22). In addition to writing her own poems and essays, and hosting The Rabble, Alice Corbin also edited an anthology of New Mexican poets called *The Turquoise Trail, An Anthology of New Mexican Poetry* (1928). In the dedication of that volume, she memorialized the true spirit of camaraderie and support that was the art colony of Santa Fe:

"This book is dedicated to the poets included in the collection, and offered to them as a record of companionships—the covers of the book now taking the place of the low-roofed adobe houses within whose walls most of the poems have, at one time or another, been shared in manuscript form" (Weigle and Fiore 29).

The poems of *Red Earth* were born of an active and deliberate involvement in the various communities of northern New Mexico. Alice and William were moved and inspired by the cultures and individuals they encountered. They sought out meaningful interactions and experiences and encouraged those around them to do the same. Alice Corbin wrote from a genuine interest in understanding her adopted hometown, and she created vivid images through her eloquent prosody. Her husband and the artists of Santa Fe did the same through visual media. It seems a fitting tribute to her, and to the art community she helped to shape, to republish her book of poetry, *Red Earth*, with images from the permanent collection of the Museum of Fine Arts.

REFERENCES

Hillerman, Tony. *The Spell of New Mexico*. Albuquerque: University of New Mexico Press, 1976.

Robertson, Edna, and Sarah Nestor. *Artists of the Canyons and Caminos, Santa Fe the Early Years*. Santa Fe: Ancient City Press, 1996.

Weigle, Marta, and Kyle Fiore. *Santa Fe and Taos: The Writer's Era, 1916–1941*. Santa Fe: Ancient City Press, 1982.

ACKNOWLEDGMENTS
By Ellen Zieselman

On a warm July day in 2001, I sat with Lois Rudnick in the Women's Board Room Gallery of the Museum of Fine Arts. We were beginning a new program at the museum, a series of informal, public interviews. Our topic for the day was women writers of the Southwest, and early in the discussion Lois read an excerpt of Alice Corbin's poem "Red Earth." As she read, all I could see in my mind was Georgia O'Keeffe's painting, *Red Hills with the Pedernal*, which is in the museum's collection. When Lois mentioned her desire to see *Red Earth* republished, I immediately thought we should republish the poems with images from our collection. This book and accompanying exhibition are the result of that brainstorm.

Some images leapt off the page, others required some real digging through our collection. In each case, we tried to match the poems with works of modern and contemporary art that were visual "equivalents" for the ideas, emotions, and sensations evoked by Alice's words. Perhaps, in a small way, the resulting duet of words and images intimates the warm exchange of ideas that made the art colony of Santa Fe such a special place for Alice Corbin and her friends.

I am indebted to Joan Tafoya, registrar at the Museum of Fine Arts, for indulging my repeated requests for access to the collection, reproductions of artworks, and general nagging; to Mary Wachs of the Museum of New Mexico Press, for her interest in the project and excellent editorial abilities; to Blair Clark, photographer for the Museum of New Mexico, for his wonderful eye; to Mary Jebsen, librarian at the Museum of Fine Arts, for her assistance; to Marsha C. Bol, director of the Museum of Fine Arts, for supporting the project from start to finish; and, of course, to Lois Rudnick, for her enthusiasm and scholarship.

INTRODUCTION
By Lois Rudnick

IN MARCH 1916, ALICE CORBIN HENDERSON traveled with her husband and daughter to a tuberculosis sanatorium in the mountains of Santa Fe to live out what she believed would be the last year of her life. She was thirty-five years old. A noted poet and associate editor of *Poetry* magazine, one of the leading arts magazines of the day, she lived and worked at the heart of twentieth-century Chicago's renaissance in the arts. When she left for New Mexico, Henderson believed that she was going from the warm center of a world that revolved around her decision-making to the ragged edge of the universe. In her haunting words, "I had been thrown out into the desert to die, like a piece of old scrap-iron, or a rusty Ford. My baggage . . . was a night-gown and a shroud, a Bible and a copy of Rabelais; the latter a parting gift from a friend who thought laughter would be curative, as it was."[1]

Henderson did not die within the year, and she remained in New Mexico until her death in 1949. Like many intellectuals, academics, artists, businessmen, and professionals who flocked to the mountains of the West and Southwest in the early twentieth century to seek a cure for one of the world's most debilitating and lethal diseases, she survived beyond expectation. "'I thought,'" she later said in an interview, "'that I was coming to a desolate exile, and I found a new world of beauty.'"[2]

Unlike most, Henderson helped to construct the place that brought her the breath of new life, both literally and creatively.

Henderson's impact on northern New Mexico occurred at several levels. She brought prominent poets to Santa Fe, such as Robert Frost, Carl Sandburg, Vachel Lindsay, and Witter Bynner. She mentored poets who moved to Santa Fe and became part of her social circle, working with some of them to found a regional press. She published numerous articles and reviews and edited books that reflect New Mexico's multicultural tradition of poetry. Her agenda was to put the literature and arts of the Southwest on the larger cultural map of the United States, an agenda that sometimes contributed to New Mexico's romantic image as "the land of enchantment." She helped to organize and raise funds for groups that collected and promoted Hispano and Native American cultural practices and productions, including the Spanish Colonial Arts Society, the New Mexico Association of Indian Affairs, and the Indian Arts Fund.

THE CHICAGO YEARS

Henderson was born in St. Louis, Missouri, on April 16, 1881. By the time she was three years old, she had lost her two younger brothers, and her mother to tuberculosis. Thereafter, she moved about, living with relatives in Virginia, Kansas, Indiana, and Illinois. In 1895, she attended Hyde Park High School in Chicago. In her third year there, Alice published her first book of poetry, *Linnet Songs* (1898). The slim volume of poems, written in the high Victorian mode, is primarily of interest for the ambition it suggests on the part of a young Midwestern woman at the turn of the twentieth century. Alice's entrance into the University of Chicago in 1899 gave further evidence of her ambition to follow a literary career.

During this time she lived with her high school English teacher, Harriet Brainard, whose home was a meeting place for the literati of the city. In 1902, suffering from chest inflammation, she moved to New Orleans, her mother's family home, and entered Sophie Newcomb College. Here she began her professional career as a journalist, writing book reviews for the *New Orleans Times-Picayune*, which gave her entrée, on her return to Chicago in 1903, to write reviews for the *Chicago Tribune* (Pearce 5).

Alice met her future and lifelong husband, William Penhallow Henderson, in 1904 when she rented a studio at the Academy of Fine Arts. An art teacher who grew up on the outskirts of Boston and descended from an old Yankee family, he was just beginning to make his mark as a painter on the Chicago art scene and had just returned from a trip to Europe where he had been introduced to the works of such leading modern artists as Cézanne and Whistler. At the time he and Alice met in the summer of 1904, Henderson was preparing for a sketching trip in Mexico and Arizona, during which he would become very much taken with the physical and cultural landscapes of the American Southwest. The Hendersons were married in the fall of 1905. Two years later, Alice gave birth to their only child, Alice Oliver.

The Henderson marriage seems to have been one of loving camaraderie, stimulated, as their daughter put it, by "mutual cross-pollination, which is evidenced by the fact that poets wrote letters to her father, and artists to her mother" (Nestor 4). They worked together on several joint projects over the years, including woodcuts and lithographs that William created for two children's books Alice published and his illustrations for her last published book, *Brothers of Light* (1937), a respectful portrait of the Penitente brotherhood, the religious society of laymen that served the rural communities of northern New Mexico. The Hendersons' métiers enriched one another—Alice widening William's sphere as she became more central to the New Poetry movement; William broadening Alice's understanding of the intimate relationship between modern poetry and modern art. It was no accident that Alice came to think of poetry as a "visual" medium.

Although in her lifetime Alice Corbin's books of poetry were published without illustration, it is fitting to the cultural moment in which she lived and worked that her poetry be paired with works of art, as in this new edition. For the birth of modern American culture, especially in the cities of New York and Chicago, gave rise to new drama, new poetry, new dance, new art and architecture, the growth of new cultural institutions, and to a rich dialogue in which painters, architects, novelists, and poets influenced each other across the arts. Their common denominator was the desire to break down conventions that defined art as a representation of some already established reality, one that typically reflected the interests of a powerful elite whose tastes were primarily limited to European and Euro-American high art. They called for poetry and painting that would create the world anew—that was original and fresh in vocabulary, self-expressive rather than imitative, and suggestive rather than definitive in meaning.

POETRY MAGAZINE

In the fall of 1912, Harriet Monroe, on a mission to begin a magazine for European and American poets who wrote in the modern vein, invited Alice to be the associate editor for her new journal, *Poetry*, a position that Alice held until 1922. During that same year, Alice published her second book of poetry, *The Spinning Woman of the Sky*, which showed a marked improvement in style over her early adolescent work but was still derivative of classical European forms and ideas. One poem in the collection speaks compellingly of her anxieties about being a woman poet:

> "Daphne"
> What greater grief could be
> Than to be born a poet—and a woman!
> To have to mind the trivial daily tasks
> That bind the heart from revery and dream,
> Or else to earn the scorn of the whole world! . . . (49)

In December 1912, Alice published the following poem in *Poetry*, speaking in an altogether different voice about her aspirations to continue the legacy of America's great poet of democracy, Walt Whitman:

> "America"
> *I hear America singing. . . .*
> And the great prophet passed,
> Serene, clear and untroubled
> Into the silence vast.
>
> When will the master-poet
> Rise, with vision strong,
> To mold her manifold music
> Into a living song? (81)

Between these contradictory desires, Henderson would live her life as a mother, wife, poet, mentor, neighbor, and community activist, perhaps never resolving her conflicting desires to be the female Walt Whitman and to serve the needs of others before her own. It is a telling mark of her ambivalence that she used her birth name, Corbin, when she published poetry and her married name when she wrote prose. Alice's desire to be a major poet was also complicated by the tuberculosis that brought her to New Mexico and flared up again at least once in her early years of living there.

During the 1910s, Henderson was much better known for her editorial work than for her poetry. She was part of a cohort of women editors who shaped the modern canon in literature. As Jayne Marek has noted in her book, *Women Editing Modernism:* "*Poetry* introduced and printed nearly every major figure in twentieth-century poetry," including Ezra Pound, Robert Frost, T. S. Eliot, William Carlos Williams, Wallace Stevens, and Carl Sandburg, along with a substantial number of women poets. The magazine "served as a forum for critical debate on a number of fundamental aesthetic issues. . . . In no small way, literary modernism was introduced into America as a result of Monroe's and Henderson's cooperative work in blending their critical skills with the raw materials of modern poetry" (21, 47).

Henderson wrote some eighty-five editorials and dozens of book reviews and essays for *Poetry* and other avant-garde magazines of the time. Her voice was bold, witty, and assured in staking out a position on several national cultural debates: the worth of American poetry; the value of regional poets from the Midwest and the Southwest; the importance of teaching modern poetry in the university English curriculum; and the necessary inclusion of ethnic literatures in the formation of an American literary tradition. In her autobiography, Monroe recalled Alice as "a pitiless reader of manuscripts; nothing stodgy or imitative would get by her finely shifting intelligence" (317). The following excerpt from Henderson's January 1915 *Poetry* editorial, "Contemporary Poetry and the Universities," underscores Monroe's point:

"Why is it that the college literary courses establish no direct contact with modern life in so far as poetry is concerned? . . . A scientific department conducted as a literary department is conducted, with no consideration of the achievements of the last thirty years, would be a disgrace to any college. . . . College students in literary courses remind one of rows of bleaching celery, banked and covered with earth; they are so carefully protected from any coloring contact with the ideas of the living present" (176–77).

Henderson's fierce advocacy of modern poetry as a kind of fifth estate that could bring "leadership" as worthy as "the elected governors and United States senators" to the "national scrimmage" over the country's most valuable resources came from her profound belief that "there is never any divorce between life and art, because art *is* life."[3] She was a leading voice among modernists who wanted to break down this false distinction, harbored by those who believed the arts should be a preserve of the few. She brought that synergy with her to New Mexico, where businessmen and civic boosters were laying the groundwork to make the arts one of the main attractions in the economic revitalization of Santa Fe. By 1916, a growing community of painters, architects, poets, fiction writers, and historians mingled and influenced one another's ideas and projects. The Henderson home would become one of their important meeting places.

EARLY YEARS IN SANTA FE

Henderson gave up a good deal in coming to Santa Fe— her relationship with *Poetry* magazine and Harriet Monroe began a long descent during which time she became increasingly unable to have her editorial voice carry weight. But she gained an incalculable immensity of new experience and knowledge that aided in her physical and mental healing and brought her to her creative heights as a poet. The same was true for her husband. William seemingly went to New Mexico without protest, yet he must have felt that he was giving up a great deal in moving to a remote city that could not provide him with the infrastructure of sponsors, dealers, and galleries he relied on for commissions and to sell his work. Like Alice's, however, his career took on positive new directions that led not only to his creating a more vibrant painterly aesthetic but also to developing his talents as a muralist, builder, and furniture maker. He became, in the process, a major contributor to the Pueblo revival style that influenced the public and private buildings of Santa Fe during the 1920s and 1930s.

The Hendersons experienced an early harbinger of their and their town's futures when they arrived at Sunmount Sanitorium, one of the most successful of the some forty tuberculosis sanatoria in New Mexico. (Alice spent her first year in Santa Fe at the sanatorium—her family living nearby—and returned in 1921 for another stay.) There its director, Dr. Frank E. Mera, tried to create a homey atmosphere enriched with cultural activities and interactions with the local community, in sharp contrast to the militarylike and isolated sanatoria that had been built across the United States in the late nineteenth and early twentieth centuries. With its integration of the arts, business, and philanthropy, Sunmount was a model for the civic culture of Santa Fe.

An active member of many cultural organizations in Santa Fe, Mera brought visiting writers, artists, and archaeologists to the sanatorium and supported the creation and performance of poetry and theater among the patients. Poet Witter Bynner, who spent time at Sunmount when he was ill with the flu during his first visit to Santa Fe in 1922, recalled that "Doctors, nurses, servants, and patients were all, in those years, easy comrades. . . . Alice brewed her own coffee, and we would gather nightly in her room for gay, swift talk and forbidden cigarettes. Now and then we would enjoy in our coffee cups a fill or two of Taos Lightning, that fiery corn whiskey which we keg-rolled in the backs of our cars" ("Alice Corbin Henderson: An Appreciation" 37).

In 1916 Santa Fe had a population of some 7000, predominantly Hispanos. The Hendersons' first years were as the only Anglos living in a neighborhood of Hispanos whose lives they participated in on the most mundane and intimate levels. They learned the daily rhythms determined by sun and rainfall, had heating wood delivered by burros, watched the earth behind their small adobe serve as a floor for the threshing of wheat, listened to men and women telling tales and singing folk songs, and participated in weddings, christenings, festivals, and wakes.

On Camino del Monte Sol, a street whose name Alice was instrumental in officially restoring to its original Spanish from the English "Telephone Road," Henderson fraternized with women who held a very different kind of power than the liberated bohemians in her Chicago milieu. There were women who did not want to be taken to the polls in 1919 because, as Señora Romero put it, "'Are the men all dead then, that you have to ask the women to vote? *Do we have to do that, too?*'" When the *dueña* of the neighborhood, Francisca Robero Y Garcia, died, she served as the model for two of Henderson's poems in her 1920 collection *Red Earth* that honor old age: "Una Anciana Mexicana" and "La Muerte de la Vieja."

In her memoir of her early years in Santa Fe, Henderson wrote, "Her death, when it came, was hard and long. She fought for her entrance into eternity as a woman fights in childbirth—it seemed the same thing."[4] In "La Muerte," she writes:

As she had fought long years ago
Through child-bed pain, now her body thin
Strove to the last with the mid-wife Death,
Till silence ushered her new life in.

The Hendersons spent a great deal of time in their first decade in Santa Fe traveling to Hispano villages in the mountains, as well as to Indian pueblos, where they befriended many. They took special interest in supporting the work of Pueblo artists such as Awa-Tsireh, who became a nationally renowned painter. Alice helped to raise money for the pueblo of Tesuque during a serious drought, fought publicly to maintain Pueblo land rights and culture, and wrote about the significance of native ceremonial art and song in and of themselves as well as for the inspiration they could provide Anglo writers who were invested in creating a national poetry.

William Penhallow Henderson
and Alice Corbin Henderson,
Taos, New Mexico, 1932.
Will Connell, photographer.
Courtesy Museum of New Mexico.

RED EARTH

If, as recent scholars have pointed out, Henderson's editorial contributions to *Poetry* have been under-recognized, so too has been her *Red Earth: Poems of New Mexico* (1920). The book marks a significant moment in the history of modern American poetry, both because of its aesthetic power and because the poems selected for it made an important contribution to the culture wars that were occurring over the formation of the modern poetry canon in the early twentieth century. *Red Earth* reflects the mediating role that Henderson played between her high modernist colleagues, such as Ezra Pound and Wallace Stevens, and such low modernist colleagues as Vachel Lindsay and Carl Sandburg, between those who believed the majority of American readers were "dolts" not worth catering to and those who strove to create a democratic poetry that spoke to ordinary men and women.[5]

In its capacious understanding of modern poetry, *Red Earth* was a radical book for its time. The book includes original imagist poems and traditional folk songs; poems written in the style of Indian songs and Hispanic ballads; and rhymed and free verse. Henderson's inclusion of a diversity of voices, forms, and styles and her intermingling of the natural and human provided important lessons for her fellow Americans in cultural pluralism and environmental awareness, including the fact that Spanish is an American language that should not necessarily require translation. Most of these poems were first published in *Poetry* magazine. They contrast starkly with the esoteric poetry Ezra Pound argued that she and Monroe should be publishing, most of it of European origin.[6]

Henderson clearly understood *Red Earth*'s significance, and she tried to keep it in print throughout the rest of her life, although it was only reprinted once, in 1921. According to her publisher's letters, some 1000 copies were printed and sold at $1.50, from which Alice earned $500 in royalties, a generous share of her publisher's receipts. She worked aggressively to control the book's design and distribution, including sending her publisher, Ralph Fletcher Seymour, shards of red clay from Inscription Rock near Zuni so he could match the color for the book's cover. She provided him with mailing lists from various poetry magazines and wrote publicity copy for the book; convinced him to print posters for bookstores and cards for newsstands; and exhorted him to take advantage of the Christmas trade in Santa Fe, "such as it is." After the book's second printing, Henderson asked him to make slips with press notices and a subscription blank that she could give to stores in Santa Fe to send out with their bills.[7]

Everyone and everything speaks in Henderson's *Red Earth*: The land, the sky, stones, dust-whorls, old and young women and men, Indians and Hispanos, in an equivalency that values no one age, gender, class, race, species, or genre. Of course, this does not mean that Henderson's attempt to speak for Native and Hispano Americans through her interpretations and translations of their songs is uncontroversial. While no one is likely to complain when she speaks for New Mexico hills that "Are spotted like lizards," critics often yell "foul" when Euro-American poets like Henderson use their culturally dominant position to speak for the marginalized and oppressed.[8] We have to acknowledge the validity of this criticism at the same time that we must also read these texts within the time frame in which they were written and against the cultures of privilege they were trying to expand and, in some cases, overturn.

In his book *The Imagist Poem*, William Pratt provides a broad framework for understanding the historic moment of Henderson's *Red Earth*: "It remains a strange but striking fact that the creative moment of modern poetry coincided with the destructive moment of modern history. For it was during the decade between 1910 and 1920, when the First World War was being fought in Europe, that the battle for a new poetic style was being fought in England and America" (19). Henderson experienced this battle at the most visceral level of her being, in her simultaneous struggle to heal her lungs and to maintain her position in the world of modern poetry after she and her family moved to Santa Fe.

As Henderson became "firmly rooted as a pinyon tree" in northern New Mexico,[9] she, like many other modernist writers and artists who moved there, became more conservative in style. This was partly due to the insistence of the landscape but also to her growing appreciation for indigenous cultural forms. She worshiped the New Mexico sun, which she believed helped to restore her to health. As she writes in "Candle-Light and Sun" in *Red Earth*:

> The sunlight is enough,
> And the earth sucking life from the sun.

The physical restoration of her life was accompanied by a new knowledge of the dignity of daily life that she learned from her Indian and Hispano neighbors. If she came increasingly to value Indian and Hispano folkways and folk arts during her years in Santa Fe, it was because their religious and aesthetic expressions were directly related to what she came to believe were the most important aspects of human life—loving, preparing food, rejoicing in the harvest, story-telling, caring for the sick, and respecting the old.

In her interpretation of a Chippewa song that she titles "Parting," Henderson conveys the moving solace of a husband to the wife with whom he has lived for many years:

> Though I go from you to die,
> We shall both lie down
> At the foot of the hill, and sleep.

In a quite different vein, "Una Anciana Mexicana," whose ordinary life Henderson describes as an "epic," relishes the pleasures of old age because of her freedom from domestic chores:

> Though one have sons and friends of one's own,
> It's better at last to live alone.[10]

To fully appreciate the context in which Henderson domesticated modern poetry, one must understand her references to the wider world in which she wrote her poetry. The "Red" in *Red Earth* refers not only to the obvious color of the clay, which is native to the soil of northern New Mexico that once belonged to "Red Man," but also to the blood-soaked world where thirteen million soldiers and civilians recently had died. As her friend, the poet Haniel Long, wrote after World War II, remembering his first encounter with these poems after World War I: "Reading the Red Earth poems in the atmosphere of postwar Europe, I could respond to their undertones; and reading them today in the bleak world of East-West tension, I respond anew to their impact. The graver the moment in one's personal life or in one's world, the more these poems have to give" ("Alice Corbin Henderson: An Appreciation" 69).

Henderson's opening untitled poem boldly asserts her postwar agenda as she describes the northern New Mexico landscape in specifically female terms, contrasting the desert and the city in terms of a male/female dichotomy that offers a new way of thinking about the metaphor of land as woman:

> Here is the desert of silence, . . .
> An old, old woman who mumbles her beads
> And crumbles to stone.

The city is youthful, strident, aggressive, gigantic, and noisy—the prototypical attributes of the American male who seeks to transform the landscape to match his visions. To be more specific, it is Carl Sandburg's city, "hog-butcher to the world." Sandburg was one of Henderson's most important protégés whose first book of poetry, *Chicago Poems*, she titled and helped to get published.[11]

When Henderson projects her human consciousness onto the landscape, she does so in order to "think" or "feel" as the land does, not in order to change it. Space, time, volume, light, sky, and wind often take the place of human will and passion. She does not assume that Euro-Americans possessed a land that was "virgin" before they settled it. The first titled poem of her book, "Red Earth," restores the land to its original inhabitants:

> This valley is not ours, nor these mountains,
> Nor the names we give them — . . .

In "Three Men Entered the Desert Alone," Alice recounts her husband's possession by the land:

> His soul extended and touched the sky,
> His old life dropped as a dream that is past, . . .[12]

"Los Conquistadores" and "A Song from Old Spain" are revisionist histories of Villagrá's triumphalist epic, "The History of New Mexico," calling into question, through voice, theme, and choice of meter, the Spanish conquest of the Southwest. In the first, three soldiers lament that they came expecting easy wealth only to find a harsh and lonely death. In the second, a young soldier about to embark for the New World promises to immortalize the love he leaves behind. She replies that she has no interest in "gold wrung from slaves" and wants only himself as her treasure. Henderson carries the theme of true versus false gold into her next poem, "In the Desert." New Mexico has divorced her from the "stream of money . . . flowing down Fifth Avenue" and substituted the "eternal gold" of "intense life" that thrives in the seemingly sterile desert.

Unfortunately that new life also includes the romanticized Mexican—"a herd-boy on the horizon" who works while she watches. Such moments occur rarely in these poems, which are more striking for their lack of sentimentality, but they do occur, as when Henderson ends her charming ballad of the woodcutter "Pedro Montoya of Arroyo Hondo" with the comment that

> With a burro to ride and a burro to drive,
> There is hardly a man so rich alive.

Pedro might have been quite happy to trade his burro for a Ford car, which would have made his work life a lot easier. When Petrolino laments the loss of tradition due to the men leaving home to "work in the mines of Colora'o" and the young girls spending money on big hats and velvet instead of on their wedding trousseaux, we can empathize with Henderson's identification with her older Hispano neighbors. At the same time we must remember that the men who left home to work had little choice—in the 1920s northern New Mexico's economy was beginning a long, slow decline—while the young girls engaged in Anglo consumer culture were exercising a form of freedom of personal choice.

Henderson is more convincing when she embraces the land as a lover, one she does not master or allow herself to be mastered by. The land she loves has an erotically charged energy that courses through human and nonhuman alike. The immediacy of her relationships with nature is sometimes preferable to the more consuming demands of human love, as she writes in "Sunlight":

Not love, not the intense moment of passion,
Not birth, is as poignant
As the sudden flash that passes
Like light reflected in a mirror
From nature to us.

Henderson transforms this flow of energy into images that bring a freshness and vitality to her poetry rarely found in her other works. The "Dust-Whorl" created by the wind is the "Faint spiral of lives" lived there, for nothing is ever lost in the desert. "My body flows like water through the stream in the canyon" celebrates what Freud called our "polymorphous perversity," the bundle of impulses we were before being locked into our human classifications by species and gender.

When Henderson writes her version of another Chippewa song she titled "Listening":

The noise of passing feet
On the prairie—
Is it men or gods
Who come out of the silence?

it is as though she were talking to Ezra Pound, demonstrating to him the ways in which Indian song is a source for the poetry revolution he announced in his 1912 "*Imagiste*" manifesto. Here he asserted that the language of poetry should be clear, direct, and exact, rooted in images that integrate mind and matter and give birth to new modes of consciousness: "'an image is that which presents an intellectual and emotional complex in an instant of time . . . which gives the sense of sudden liberation; that sense of freedom from time limits and space limits; that sense of sudden growth, which we experience in the presence of the greatest works of art'" (Pratt 26).

The source of Henderson's admiration for Indian song came from the fact that its symbols were generated out of the necessities of life and were never, as she put it, merely "decorative." However problematic it is that Henderson took Indian songs out of their particular tribal contexts and interpreted them for her own purposes, as she did with the Chippewa songs translated by Frances Densmore which were the basis for seven of her Indian poems in *Red Earth*, she never claimed to be doing otherwise. When she first published these poems in *Poetry* magazine, she noted that she took from Indian songs a "key-note—which is often not more than a phrase, a single image, with variations of musical inflection and repetition—and expanded it very slightly." She acknowledged that "any addition whatever is taking liberties with the originals but I have tried to keep strictly within the spirit of them."[13]

Certainly Henderson wrote as an outsider at several removes from the original songs she interpreted. As Michael Castro reminds us in his book *Interpreting the Indian*, she did not write Indian poetry; she wrote poetry about Indians. At the same time, however, she recognized and attempted to emulate many of the characteristics that ethnomusicologists attribute to Indian ceremonial song. As Castro explains, its purpose is "to make and shape the world through the power and magic of the word"; its use of brevity is "based on imagistic and symbolic usages"; and its use of repetition allows the individual to share "'the quality of consciousness that characterizes most orders of being.'" Most importantly, it is intended as an "'accumulation of power' that humans "can harness and use . . . " (34–35).

The techniques and intentions of Indian song parallel Imagism's desire to strip away unnecessary detail in an attempt to arrive at unornamented truth. The Western world had demonstrated during World War I how easy it was to abuse language in service to destruction and death. Henderson was like many of her elite modernist colleagues in her postwar repudiation of the industrial city and in her search for eternal truths that were never old. But she was not at all interested in an "art for the privileged's sake" that made poetry inaccessible to the multitudes. She wanted poems that were an "accumulation of power" that could heal emotional and social wounds and provide a standard of national values that honored diverse cultural voices and traditions.

The inspiration Henderson received from the high deserts of New Mexico energized the poems she included in *Red Earth* on behalf of these beliefs. At their best, they support the evaluation of her work made by her biographer, T. M. Pearce: "In *Red Earth* she found a new and authentic voice as a poet, not an Indian voice nor a Spanish voice nor an Anglo voice, but a personal voice expressing the lives of the peoples among whom she lived and interpreting their experiences and her own in the immediacy of regional color and speech" (21).

POSTSCRIPT

Henderson's life after the publication of *Red Earth* was a richly productive one, although her output of poetry was slim over the next nineteen years. She devoted herself primarily to editorial and community work connected to her desire to promote folk poetry and regional cultural interests on a national level. These efforts included her writing an introduction for Howard Thorp's expanded volume of *Songs of the Cowboy* and the foreword for Mary Van Stone's translation of *Spanish Folk Songs of New Mexico*.

Alice Corbin, 1932.
Will Connell, photographer.
Harwood Museum of
University of New Mexico.

She also edited the first major book of New Mexico poetry, *The Turquoise Trail,* which included the work of locals as well as national and international notables, such as Mary Austin, Mabel Luhan, and D. H. Lawrence.

During the 1930s, Alice was one of the founding members of "The Poet's Round-Up," a takeoff on the rodeo, during which poets came out of imitation "chutes" and read poems to raise money on behalf of the New Mexico Association of Indian Affairs. She also joined with four poet friends to found a cooperative, the Writers' Editions, devoted to publishing regional writers. They produced fourteen books between 1933 and 1939, including Alice's last book of poetry, *The Sun Turns West* (1933). In the late 1930s, she served as the first curator of the Museum of Navaho Ceremonial Art, later the Wheelwright Museum of the American Indian, which was designed by her husband and built under the auspices of Mary Cabot Wheelwright.

When the Works Progress Administration hired writers to create travel guides to the States in order to promote tourism during the Great Depression, Henderson was asked to write the section on New Mexico literature. She starts her section with the then almost unheard of acknowledgment that the state's literary tradition (and by extension the national literary tradition) "begins with the orally transmitted myths, legends and rituals of the

Indians who were native to the soil when the Spaniards came" and with "the old Spanish chronicles of exploration and conquest" which "rank among the great original adventure books of the world" (130).

In a heartfelt "Appreciation" of Henderson's contributions to her beloved community, written by Santa Fe writers shortly before she died, Ruth Laughlin noted: "In Santa Fe we value Alice Corbin as a good citizen, a distinguished poet and a beloved neighbor" ("Alice Corbin Henderson: An Appreciation" 66). Henderson might have wished to be remembered as a poet of national renown, but it is a fitting tribute to her sense of civic responsibility and to her humanity that Laughlin gave all three of these roles the same value.

NOTES

1. "Early Impressions of Santa Fe, 1916–1934," TS, n.p., Box 22, folder 15, Alice Corbin Henderson Collection, Harry Ransom Center, University of Texas, Austin; cited hereafter as ACH.

2. Henderson is quoted by Hildegarde Hawthorne in *The Literary Digest International Book Review*, 1926 or 1927, "Notebook: Reviews and Articles, 1914–1938," Box 18, folder 10, ACH.

3. For the argument that poetry was as important as politics (and football), see "Vachel Lindsay's Plans for Poets," *Chicago Herald Tribune*, July 17, 1915, Box, 29, folder 2, ACH. The article encapsulates a manifesto that Lindsay and Henderson read at the annual dinner of the Poetry Society of America, in which they presented their program "to make the ninety million American people aware that there is at least one living poet to every million inhabitants"; Henderson, "Science and Art Again," *Poetry* vol. 1, no. 4 (1920): 205. In this editorial, Henderson quarrels with the noted engineer, Charles Steinmetz, who in an article had referred to poetry's "irrelevance to the modern world." Henderson would undoubtedly be pleased to know that the magazine she helped to start has maintained its position as one of the best-regarded magazines of poetry in the nation. In October 2002, it received a bequest of $100 million from a longtime admirer, Ruth Lilly. Given Henderson's tough

editorial standards, she might have been more impressed by the fact that the magazine consistently refused to publish Lilly's poetry.

4. "Early Impressions of Santa Fe," Box 22, folder 15, ACH.

5. The "mass of dolts" is a phrase used by Ezra Pound at the end of his poem, "To Whistler—American," as quoted by Monroe, p. 289: "You and Abe Lincoln, from that mass of dolts. . . ."

6. Among Henderson's papers is a folder of requests by a dozen poetry editors asking her permission to reprint copies of her poems in their high school and college anthologies of regional and national literature. Most of the poems requested had been published in *Red Earth*.

7. See Henderson's correspondence with her publisher Ralph Fletcher Seymour, ACH, which includes a folder containing twenty-two reviews of *Red Earth* from newspapers in Boston, New York, Chicago, and San Francisco, and such magazines as the *New Republic, Literary Digest, Bookman,* and *Le Monde Nouveau.*

8. For criticisms of Euro-American appropriations and patronage of Indian and Hispano cultures see the work of Michael Castro, Sarah Deutsch, Margaret Jacobs, and Charles Montgomery.

9. The quote comes from her letter of resignation as Associate Editor of *Poetry,* reprinted in *El Palacio,* vol. 13, no. 9 (1922): 110.

10. With one exception, I have not been able to locate the "traditional" songs in *Red Earth* that Alice wrote Harriet Monroe in 1919 that she was translating. She seems to identify those she translated by supplying subtitles (e.g., "From the Spanish") or by crediting her sources in the endnotes. "El Coyotito" was first published by Charles F. Lummis in his *Land of Poco Tiempo* (1904). According to the noted literary folklorist Enrique R. Lamadrid, both Lummis and Corbin present the gist of the original New Mexican folk song, in terms of acknowledging the lusty character of coyote, but their translations include some misconstructions of the original Spanish and some faniciful additions of their own in attempting to create rhymed English verse. I would like to thank Dr. Lamadrid for his help with the translations.

11. Alan Filreis makes the point about Henderson's poem responding to the "muscular urbanism" of Sandburg's Chicago, p. 6.

12. During the 1980s, the Hendersons' daughter, Alice Rossin, told me that this poem was based on a trip her father took.

13. Densmore was an ethnomusicologist who worked for fifty years collecting and recording Indian songs throughout the Midwest and the West; Henderson, "Aboriginal Poetry," *Poetry*, vol. 9, no. 5 (1917): 256.

BIBLIOGRAPHY

"Alice Corbin Henderson: An Appreciation." *New Mexico Quarterly Review,* vol. 19, no. 1(1949): 34–79.

Bell, David. "A Biographical Sketch," in *William Penhallow Henderson: Master Colorist of Santa Fe.* Phoenix: Phoenix Art Museum, 1984.

Castro, Michael. *Interpreting the Indian: Twentieth-Century Poets and the Native American.* Albuquerque: University of New Mexico Press, 1983.

Deutsch, Sarah. *No Separate Refuge: Culture, Class, and Gender on an Anglo-Hispanic Frontier in the American West, 1880–1940.* New York: Oxford University Press, 1987.

Filreis, Alan. "Voicing the Desert of Silence: Stevens' Letters to Alice Corbin Henderson," *The Wallace Stevens Journal,* vol. 12, issue 1 (1988): 3–20.

Henderson, Alice Corbin. *The Spinning Woman of the Sky.* Chicago: Ralph Fletcher Syemour, 1912.

_____. *Red Earth: Poems of New Mexico.* Chicago: Ralph Fletcher Seymour, 1920.

_____. "Introduction," *Songs of the Cowboy,* N. Howard Thorp, ed.; enlarged edition. Boston: Houghton Mifflin Co., 1921; originally published, 1908.

_____, ed. *The Turquoise Trail, An Anthology of New Mexico Poetry.* Boston: Houghton Mifflin Co., 1928.

_____. "Foreword," *Spanish Folk Songs of New Mexico,* translated by Mary Van Stone. Chicago: Ralph Fletcher Seymour, 1928.

_____. *The Sun Turns West.* Santa Fe: Writers' Editions, 1933.

_____. *Brothers of Light: The Penitentes of the Southwest.* New York: Harcourt, Brace and Co., 1937.

_____. "Literature," in *The WPA Guide to 1930s New Mexico.* Tucson: University of Arizona Press, 1989, pp.

130–140; originally published as *New Mexico: A Guide to the Colorful State* (1940).

Jacobs, Margaret. *Engendered Encounters: Feminism and Pueblo Cultures, 1879–1934.* Lincoln: University of Nebraska Press, 1999.

La Farge, John Pen. *Turn Left at the Sleeping Dog: Scripting the Santa Fe Legend, 1920–1955.* Albuquerque: University of New Mexico Press, 2001.

Marek, Jayne. *Women Editing Modernism: 'Little' Magazines & Literary History.* Louisville: University of Kentucky Press, 1995.

Monroe, Harriet. *A Poet's Life: Seventy Years in a Changing World.* New York: AMS Press, 1969.

Montgomery, Charles. *The Spanish Redemption: Heritage, Power, and Loss on New Mexico's Upper Rio Grande.* Berkeley: University of California Press, 2002.

Nestor, Sarah, ed. *El Palacio,* vol. 93, no. 2 (1987), Special Issue on William Penhallow Henderson.

Pearce, T. M. *Alice Corbin Henderson: A New Voice in Poetry.* Southwest Writer's Series, no. 21. Austin: Steck-Vaughn, 1969.

Pratt, William. *The Imagist Poem: Modern Poetry in Miniature.* Ashland, OR: Storyline Press, 1963.

Rudnick, Lois. "Re-Naming the Land: Anglo Expatriate Women in New Mexico," in *The Desert Is No Lady: Southwestern Landscapes in Women's Writing and Art.* Eds. Vera Norwood and Jan Monk. New Haven: Yale University Press, 1987; University of Arizona Press, 1997.

Spidle, Jack Jr. "Coughing and Spitting in New Mexico History," in *Essays in Twentieth-Century New Mexico History.* Ed. Judith Boyce DeMark. Albuquerque: University of New Mexico Press, 1994, pp. 169–180.

Wilson, Chris. *The Myth of Santa Fe: Creating a Modern Regional Tradition.* Albuquerque: University of New Mexico Press, 1997.

RED EARTH

After the roar, after the fierce modern music
Of rivets and hammers and trams,
After the shout of the giant,
Youthful and brawling and strong
Building the cities of men,
Here is the desert of silence,
Blinking and blind in the sun—
An old, old woman who mumbles her beads
And crumbles to stone.

GEORGIA O'KEEFFE

Red Hills with the Pedernal, 1936
Oil on linen
Museum of New Mexico, Museum of Fine Arts
Bequest of Helen Miller Jones, 1986

RED EARTH

EL RITO DE SANTA FE

This valley is not ours, nor these mountains,
Nor the names we give them — they belong,
They, and this sweep of sun-washed air,
Desert and hill and crumbling earth,
To those who have lain here long years
And felt the soak of the sun
Through the red sand and crumbling rock,
Till even their bones were part of the sun-steeped
      valley;
How many years we know not, nor what names
They gave to antelope, wolf, or bison,
To prairie dog or coyote,
To this hill where we stand,
Or the moon over your shoulder . . .

Let us build a monument to Time
That knows all, sees all, and contains all,
To whom these bones in the valley are even as we
      are:
Even Time's monument would crumble
Before the face of Time,
And be as these white bones
Washed clean and bare by the sun . . .

ERNEST KNEE

Sand Hills Near Abiquiu, NM, 1935
Gelatin-silver photograph
Museum of New Mexico, Museum of Fine Arts
Museum purchase, Fine Arts Acquisition Funds, 1988

LOS CONQUISTADORES

What hills, what hills,
my old true love?
—Old Song

What hills are these against the sky,
What hills so far and cold?
These are the hills we have come to find,
Seeking the yellow gold.

What hills, what hills so dark and still,
What hills so brown and dry?
These are the hills of this desert land
Where you and I must die.

Oh, far away is gay Seville,
And far are the hills of home,
And far are the plains of old Castile
Beneath the blue sky's dome.

The bells will ring in fair Seville,
And folks go up and down,
And no one knows where our bones are laid
In this desert old and brown.

What hills, what hills so dark and cold,
What hills against the sky?
These are the last hills you shall see
Before you turn to die.

EARL STROH

Sand Storm, 1951
Oil on masonite panel
Museum of New Mexico, Museum of Fine Arts
Gift of the Helene Wurlitzer Foundation of New Mexico, 1964

THREE MEN ENTERED THE DESERT ALONE

Three men entered the desert alone.
But one of them slept like a sack of stone
As the wagon toiled and plodded along,
And one of them sang a drinking song
He had heard at the bar of The Little Cyclone.

Then he too fell asleep at last,
While the third one felt his soul grow vast
As the circle of sand and alkali.
His soul extended and touched the sky,
His old life dropped as a dream that is past,

As the sand slipped off from the wagon wheel—
The shining sand from the band of steel,
While the far horizon widened and grew
Into something he dimly felt he knew,
And had always known, that had just come true.

His vision rested on ridges of sand,
And a far-off horseman who seemed to stand
On the edge of the world —in an orange glow
Rising to rose and a lavender tone,
With an early star in a turquoise band.

And his spirit sang like a taper slim,
As the slow wheels turned on the desert's rim
Through the wind-swept stretches of sand and sky;
He had entered the desert to hide and fly,
But the spell of the desert had entered him.

Three men entered the desert alone.
One of them slept like a sack of stone,
One of them reached till he touched the sky.
The other one dreamed, while the hours went by,
Of a girl at the bar of The Little Cyclone.

WILLIAM PENHALLOW HENDERSON

Landscape (Cerro Gordo Before the Sangre de Cristo Mountains), c. 1930
Oil on canvas
Museum of New Mexico, Museum of Fine Arts
Gift of P. E. R. A., 1972

A SONG FROM OLD SPAIN

What song of mine will live?
On whose lips will the words be sung
Long years after I am forgotten—
A name blown between the hills
Where some goat-herd
Remembers my love and passion?

He will sing of your beauty and my love
Though it may be in another tongue,
To a strange tune,
In a country beyond the seas—
A seed blown by the wind—
He will sing of our love and passion.

IN THE SIERRAS

Do not bring me riches
From your store in the Andes
Do not bring me treasures
From deep ocean caves.
Bring me but yourself
And I'll gladly go with you,
Bring me but yourself,
And I will not be sorry.

Do not bring me patterns
Of silks or of satins,
Do not bring me silver
Or gold wrung from slaves.
Bring me but yourself,
And my heart will rest easy,
And your head will be light
With my breast as its pillow.

Do not bring me servants
Or oxen or cattle,
Or sheep for the shearing
Or ships from the waves.
Bring me but yourself
For my share and my treasure,
Then our fortune will grow
And will never diminish.

VICTOR HIGGINS

Untitled, n.d.
Oil on canvas
Museum of New Mexico, Museum of Fine Arts
Gift of the estate of Joan Higgins Reed, 1984

IN THE DESERT

I

I have seen you, O king of the dead,
More beautiful than sunlight.

Your kiss is like quicksilver;
But I turned my face aside
Lest you should touch my lips.

In the field with the flowers
You stood darkly.

My knees trembled, and I knew
That no other joy would be like this.

But the warm field, and the sunlight,
And the few years of my girlhood
Came before me, and I cried,
Not yet!
Not yet, O dark lover!

You were patient.
 —I know you will come again.

I have seen you, O king of the dead,
More beautiful than sunlight.

GUSTAVE BAUMANN

Fifth Avenue, 1918

Color woodcut

Museum of New Mexico, Museum of Fine Arts

With funds raised by the School of American
Research, 1952

II

Here in the desert, under the cottonwoods
That keep up a monotonous wind-murmur of
     leaves,
I can hear the water dripping
Through the canals in Venice
From the oar of the gondola
Hugging the old palaces,
Beautiful old houses
Sinking quietly into decay. . . .

O sunlight—how many things you gild
With your eternal gold!
Sunlight—and night—are everlasting.

III

Once every twenty-four hours
Earth has a moment of indecision:
Shall I go on?—
Shall I keep turning?—
Is it worth while?
Everything holds its breath.
The trees huddle anxiously.
On the edge of the arroyo,
And then, with a tremendous heave,
Earth shoves the hours on towards dawn.

IV

Four o'clock in the afternoon. . . .
A stream of money is flowing down Fifth Avenue.

They speak of the fascination of New York
Climbing aboard motor-busses to look down on
     the endless play
From the Bay to the Bronx.

But it is forever the same:
There is no *life* there.
Watching a cloud on the desert,
Endlessly watching small insects crawling in and
       out of the shadow of a cactus,
A herd-boy on the horizon driving goats,
Uninterrupted sky and blown sand:
Space —volume —silence —
Nothing but life on the desert,
Intense life.

V

The hill cedars and piñons
Point upward like flames,
Like smoke they are drawn upward
From the face of the mountains.
Over the sunbaked slopes,
Patches of sun-dried adobes straggle;
Willows along the acequias in the valley
Give cool streams of green;
Beyond, on the bare hillsides,
Yellow and red gashes and bleached white paths
Give foothold to the burros,
To the black-shawled Mexican girls
Who go for water.

HOWARD NORTON COOK

Buffalo Dancers Return, 1976
Oil on canvas
Museum of New Mexico, Museum of Fine Arts
Gift of the Artist, 1982

INDIAN SONGS

LISTENING

The noise of passing feet
On the prairie—
Is it men or gods
Who come out of the silence?

BUFFALO DANCE

Strike ye our land
With curved horns!
Now with cries
Bending our bodies
Breathe fire upon us;
Now with feet
Trampling the earth,
Let your hoofs,
Thunder over us!
Strike ye our land
With curved horns!

WHERE THE FIGHT WAS

In the place where the fight was
Across the river,
In the place where the fight was
Across the river:
A heavy load for a woman
To lift in her blanket,
A heavy load for a woman
To carry on her shoulder.
In the place where the fight was
Across the river,
In the place where the fight was
Across the river:
The women go wailing
To gather the wounded,
The women go wailing
To pick up the dead.

THE WIND

The wind is carrying me round the sky;
The wind is carrying me round the sky.
My body is here in the valley —
The wind is carrying me round the sky.

COURTSHIP

When I go I will give you surely
What you will wear if you go with me;
A blanket of red and a bright girdle,
Two new moccasins and a silver necklace.
When I go I will give you surely
What you will wear if you go with me!

FEAR

The odor of death
In the front of my body,
The odor of death
Before me —

Is there any one
Who would weep for me?
My wife
Would weep for me.

PARTING

Now I go, do not weep, woman —
Woman, do not weep;
Though I go from you to die,
We shall both lie down
At the foot of the hill, and sleep.

Now I go, do not weep, woman —
Woman, do not weep;
Earth is our mother and our tent the sky.
Though I go from you to die,
We shall both lie down
At the foot of the hill, and sleep.

FRITZ SCHOLDER

Snake Dancer, 1967
Oil on board
Museum of New Mexico, Museum of Fine Arts
Gift of Mr. John B. L. Goodwin, 1969

SAND PAINTINGS

The dawn breeze
Loosens the leaves
Of the trees,
The wide sky quivers
With awakened birds.

Two blue runners
Come from the east,
One has a scarf of silver,
One flings pine-boughs
Across the sky.

Noon-day stretched
In gigantic slumber —
Red copper cliffs
Rigid in sunlight.

An old man stoops
For a forgotten faggot,
Forehead of bronze
Between white locks
Bound with a rag of scarlet.

Where one door stands open,
The female moon
Beckons to darkness
And disappears.

ALFRED STIEGLITZ

Equivalent, 1929

Gelatin-silver photo-
graph, Museum of
New Mexico, Museum
of Fine Arts

Bequest of Rebecca
Salsbury James, 1968

ALFRED STIEGLITZ

Equivalent, 1929

Gelatin-silver photo-
graph, Museum of
New Mexico, Museum
of Fine Arts

Bequest of Rebecca
Salisbury James, 1968

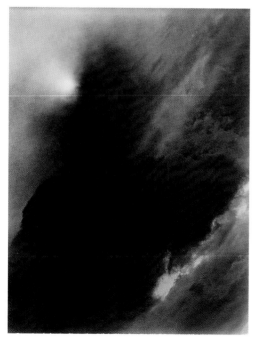

CORN-GRINDING SONG

TESUQUE PUEBLO
This way from the north
Comes the cloud,
Very blue,
And inside the cloud is the blue corn.

> *How beautiful the cloud*
> *Bringing corn of blue color!*

This way from the west
Comes the cloud,
Very yellow,
And inside the cloud is the yellow corn.

> *How beautiful the cloud*
> *Bringing corn of yellow color!*

This way from the south
Comes the cloud,
Very red,
And inside the cloud is the red corn.

> *How beautiful the cloud*
> *Bringing corn of red color!*

This way from the east
Comes the cloud,
Very white,
And inside the cloud is the white corn.

> *How beautiful the cloud*
> *Bringing corn of white color!*

How beautiful the clouds
From the north and the west
From the south and the east
Bringing corn of all colors!

(*From the Indian*)

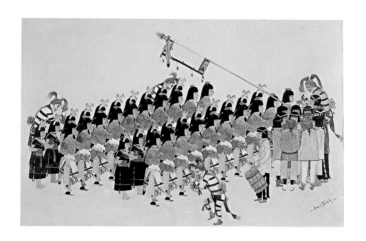

AWA-TSIREH (ALFONSO ROYBAL)

The Green Corn Ceremony at Santo Domingo, n.d.

Gouache on board

Museum of Indian Arts and Culture (Laboratory of Anthropology)

Courtesy John and Linda Comstock and The Abigail Van Vleck Charitable Trust

THE GREEN CORN DANCE

SAN ILDEFONSO

Far in the east
The gods beat
On thunder drums.

With rhythmic thud
The dancers' feet
Answer the beat
Of the thunder drums . . .

Eagle feather
On raven hair,
With bright tablita's
Turquoise glare.

Tasselled corn
Stands tall and fair
From rain-washed roots
Through lambent air . . .

Corn springs up
From the seed in the ground,
The cradled corn
By the sun is found.

Eagle feather
And turkey plume
From the wind-swept cloud
Bring rain and gloom.

Hid in the cloud
The wind brings rain
And the water-song
To the dust-parched plain.

Far in the east
The gods retreat
As the thunder drums
Grow small and sweet.

The dancers' feet
Echo the sound
As the drums grow faint
And the rain comes down.

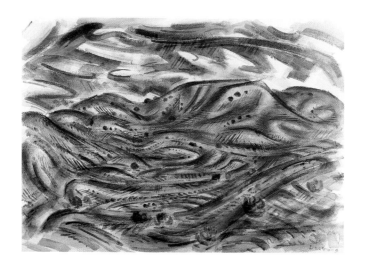

ANDREW DASBURG

Sangre de Cristo, c. 1933
Watercolor
Museum of New Mexico, Museum of Fine Arts
Gift of Mr. Edwin F. Gamble, 1980

DESERT DRIFT

SPRING

Spring has come
To the apricot boughs;
The cottonwoods
Fringe green on the branches.
Today the flood-gates are opened,
And thin streams loosed
From the high peaks of snow
To acequias in the valley.

DUST-WHORL

The wind picks up a handful of dust,
And sets it down—
Faint spiral of lives
Lived long ago on the desert.

TREES AND HORSES

Trees stand motionless among themselves,
Some are solitary.
Horses wander over wide pastures;
At night they herd closely,
Rumps hunched to the wind.

BIRD-SONG AND WIRE

The Rocky-Mountain blue-bird
Is a point of blue fire;
The meadow-lark
Sings above the hum
Of the telephone wire.

Straight and gaunt
The poles stand;
They walk stiffly
Over a thousand leagues
Of rough land.

THE WRESTLER

The tired wind creeps down the canyon
At nightfall.
By day it turns and flings itself
Against the granite face of the mountains.

FOOT-HILLS

New Mexico hills
Are spotted like lizards,
They sinuously glide and dissemble;
If you take a forked stick
You may catch one and hold it.

WAITING

More still than death
That waits a thousand years
In a new-ploughed field
Of up-turned bones;
So will I wait for you
A thousand years.

AFTERNOON

Earth tips to the west
And the hills lean backward —
Cedar-trees
Hugging the hillsides.

Smoke drifts in the valley —
The pinto sun
Nickers over the gate
Of the home corral.

CACTUS

The cactus scrawls crude hieroglyphs against the
     sky;
It reaches with twisted, inquisitive fingers
To clutch the throat of something and question
     Why.

STONE-PINE AND STREAM

The stone-pine with green branches
Stands on the brink of the canyon,
The wind whispers in the tree —
The wind lifts my hair.
Water runs with a pattern of braided and woven
     music
Through the stream in the canyon —
My body flows like water through the stream in
     the canyon.

SHADOW

A deep blue shadow falls
On the face of the mountain —
What great bird's wing
Has dropped a feather?

ELIOT PORTER

Post Office, Trampas, New Mexico, 1940

Gelatin silver photograph

Museum of New Mexico, Museum of Fine Arts

Gift of Gil Hitchcock in cooperation with the
New Mexico Council on Photography, 1984.
©1990 Amon Carter Museum, Fort Worth, Texas,
Bequest of the artist.

GOLD

Gold is under these hills;
And the wind piles sand
Through the cracks of deserted cabins.

Gold chinked over the counters,
Gold poured into the glasses,
Gold flickered and flamed
In the spendthrift gleam
Of a woman's hair . . .

Gold is under these hills,
Gold in the empty sunlight.

NIGHT

The night is dark, and the moon
Moves heavily, dragging a cross;
Penitent peaks drip, crowned with cactus;
The wind whips itself mournfully
Through the arroyos.

DESCANSO

Beside this wooden cross
By the cross of the desert cactus,
The coffin-bearers rested:
"Pray for the soul
Of Manuel Rodriguez,"
And remember
That death is the end of life.

PUEBLO

The pueblo rises under the sun-bronzed noon
As if hammered out of copper;
The sky's metallic blue
Rings in the silence.
Nothing moves but the shapes
That strain without changing.

DOUBLE

Who is this running with me
Whose shadow alone I see,
And at high noon hear only
The soft tread of his sandals?

FIESTA

The sun dances to the drums
With cottonwood boughs
On head and ankles.

The moon steps softly
In a turquoise tablita.

The stars run to pick up
The eagle feathers
Dropped by the dancers.

ANA MENDIETA

Untitled (Silueta Series), c. 1970–80
Kodak photograph
Museum of New Mexico, Museum of Fine Arts
Museum purchase, Lucy Lippard Collection

FROM THE STONE AGE

Long ago some one carved me in the semblance
      of a god.
I have forgot now what god I was meant to
      represent.
I have no consciousness now but of stone, sun-
      light, and rain;
The sun baking my skin of stone, the wind
      lifting my hair;
The sun's light is hot upon me,
The moon's light is cool,
Casting a silver-laced pattern of light and dark
Over the planes of my body:
My thoughts now are the thoughts of a stone,
My substance now is the substance of life itself;
I have sunk deep into life as one sinks into sleep;
Life is above me, below me, around me,
Moving through my pores of stone —
It does not matter how small the space you pack
      life in,
That space is as big as the universe —
Space, volume, and the overtone of volume
Move through me like chords of music,
Like the taste of happiness in the throat,
Which you fear to lose, though it may choke you —
(In the cities this is not known,
For space there is emptiness,
And time is torment) . . . . .
Since I became a stone
I have no need to remember anything —
Everything is remembered for me;
I live and I think and I dream as a stone,

In the warm sunlight, in the grey rain;
All my surfaces are touched to softness
By the light fingers of the wind,
The slow dripping of rain:
My body retains only faintly the image
It was meant to represent,
I am more beautiful and less rigid,
I am a part of space,
Time has entered into me,
Life has passed through me —
What matter the name of the god I was meant
        to represent?

LAURA GILPIN

The "He" Rain, 1946

Gelatin-silver photograph

Museum of New Mexico, Museum of Fine Arts

Museum purchase from Museum of New Mexico Foundation Grant
©1979 Amon Carter Museum, Fort Worth, Texas, Bequest of the artist.

CANDLE-LIGHT AND SUN

CANDLE-LIGHT

It might have been me in the darkened room
With the shutters closed,
Lying straight and slim
In the shuttered dusk,
In the twilight dim:
Like a silken husk
When the corn is gone,
Life withdrawn;
I am living, and she is dead —
Or is it I who have died instead?

THE MASK

Death is a beautiful white mask,
That slips over the face, when the moment comes,
To hide the happiness of the soul.

RAIN-PRAYER

A broken ploughed field
In the driving rain,
Rain driven slant-wise
Over the plain.
I long for the rain,
The dull long rain,
For farmlands and ploughlands
And cornlands again.
O grey broken skies,
You were part of my pain!

FAME

Fame is an echo
Far off, remote —
But love is a sweetness
You taste in the throat,
Friendship a comfort
When twilight falls.
But fame is an echo
Through empty halls.

SUNLIGHT

The sunlight is enough,
And the earth sucking life from the sun.
Horses in a wide field are a part of it,
Dappled and white and brown;
Trees are another kind of life,
Linked to us but not understood.
(Whoever can understand a horse or a tree
Can understand a star or a planet:
But one may feel things without understanding,
Or one may understand them through feeling.)
The simple light of the sun is enough.
One will never remember
A greater thing when one dies
Than sunlight falling aslant long rows of corn,
Or rainy days heavy with grey sullen skies.
Not love, not the intense moment of passion,
Not birth, is as poignant
As the sudden flash that passes
Like light reflected in a mirror
From nature to us.

LARRY CALCAGNO

Landscape, 1970
Acrylic on canvas
Museum of New Mexico, Museum of Fine Arts
Gift of the Gallery of Modern Art, Taos, New Mexico, 1973

THE EAGLE'S SONG

The eagle sings to the sea-gull,
"My eyes are blind with pain,
Peering into the sun's face,
As yours in the tossing main;

Yours are the depths of the sea,
Mine the fathomless sky,
Between us the tides of men
Who blossom, and fall, and die."

The eagle sings to the sea-gull,
"The world will toss and strain
Till the mountains march to the sea,
And the sea climbs back again."

The eagle sings to the sea-gull,
"The mountains wait and sleep."
And the sea-gull sings to the eagle
The old sing-song of the deep.

JOHN C. COLLIER JR.

Trampas, NM
(Grandfather Romero is 99 Years Old), 1943
Modern gelatin-silver photograph
Museum of New Mexico, Museum of Fine Arts

The Pinewood Foundation Collection, Farm Security
Admin. photographs, with additional support from
Barbara Erdman, Library of Congress, 1990

ON THE ACEQUIA MADRE

Death has come to visit us today,
He is such a distinguished visitor
Everyone is overcome by his presence —
"Will you not sit down—take a chair?"

But Death stands in the doorway, waiting to
        depart;
He lingers like a breath in the curtains.
The whole neighborhood comes to do him honor,
Women in black shawls and men in black
        sombreros
Sitting motionless against white-washed walls;
And the old man with the grey stubby beard
To whom death came,
Is stunned into silence.
Death is such a distinguished visitor,
Making even old flesh important.

But who now, I wonder, will take the old horse
        to pasture?

TOM LEA

Untitled (El Leñador), 1934
Oil on canvas
Museum of New Mexico, Museum of Fine Arts
Gift of P. E. R. A., 1979

PEDRO MONTOYA OF ARROYO HONDO

Pedro Montoya of Arroyo Hondo
Comes each day with his load of wood
Piled on two burros' backs, driving them down
Over the mesa to Santa Fe town.

He comes around by Arroyo Chamisa—
A small grey figure, as grey as his burros —
Down from the mountains, with cedar and pine
Girt about each of the burros with twine.

As patient as they are, he waits in the plaza
For someone who comes with an eye out for wood,
Then Pedro wakes up, like a bantam at dawn —
Si, Señor, si Señor—his wood is gone.

Pedro Montoya of Arroyo Hondo
Rides back on one burro and drives the other,
With a sack of blue corn-meal, tobacco and meat,
A bit to smoke and a bit to eat.

Pedro Montoya of Arroyo Hondo —
If I envied any, I'd envy him!
With a burro to ride and a burro to drive,
There is hardly a man so rich alive.

JOHN CANDELARIO

Descanso, Rio in Medio, 1936
Unique Platinum photograph
Museum of New Mexico, Museum of Fine Arts
Museum purchase, 1997

UNA ANCIANA MEXICANA

I've seen her pass with eyes upon the road —
An old bent woman in a bronze black shawl,
With skin as dried and wrinkled as a mummy's,
As brown as a cigar-box, and her voice
Like the low vibrant strings of a guitar.
And I have fancied from the girls about
What she was at their age, what they will be
When they are old as she. But now she sits
And smokes away each night till dawn comes
    round,
Thinking, beside the piñons' flame, of days
Long past and gone, when she was young — content
To be no longer young, her epic done:

    For a woman has work and much to do,
    And it's good at the last to know it's through,
    And still have time to sit alone,
    To have some time you can call your own.
    It's good at the last to know your mind
    And travel the paths that you traveled blind,
    To see each turn and even make
    Trips in the byways you did not take —
    But that, *por Dios*, is over and done,
    It's pleasanter now in the way we've come;
    It's good to smoke and none to say
    What's to be done on the coming day,
    No mouths to feed or coat to mend,
    And none to call till the last long end.
    Though one have sons and friends of one's own,
    It's better at last to live alone.
    For a man must think of food to buy,
    And a woman's thoughts may be wild and high;

But when she is young she must curb her pride,
And her heart is tamed for the child at her side.
But when she is old her thoughts may go
Wherever they will, and none to know.
And night is the time to think and dream,
And not to get up with the dawn's first gleam;
Night is the time to laugh or weep,
And when dawn comes it is time to sleep . . .

When it's all over and there's none to care,
I mean to be like her and take my share
Of comfort when the long day's done,
And smoke away the nights, and see the sun
Far off, a shrivelled orange in a sky gone black,
Through eyes that open inward and look back.

ESQUIPULA ROMERO DE ROMERO

The Black Shawl, 1933

Oil on masonite

Museum of New Mexico, Museum of Fine Arts

Museum purchase, with funds from the
Jordi M. Chilson Trust and additional support
from Friends of Contemporary Art, 1997

MADRE MARIA

From the Spanish

On the mountain Lucia
Was Madre Maria,
With book of gold.
Half was she reading,
Half praying and pleading
For sorrow foretold.

Came her son Jesus
To the mountain Lucia:
"What are you doing then,
Madre Maria?"

"Nor reading nor sleeping,
But dreaming a dream.
On Calvary's hill-top
Three crosses gleam,
Bare in the moonlight;
Your body on one
Nailed feet and hands,
O my dear little son!"

"Be it so, be it so,
O mi Madre Maria!"

Who says this prayer
Three times a day
Will find Heaven's doors
Opened always,
And Hell's doors shut
Forever and aye....

Amen, Jesus!

JOHN CANDELARIO

Penitente Cross and Chapel, San Pedro, 1937
Unique platinum photograph
Museum of New Mexico, Museum of Fine Arts
Museum purchase, 1997

CUNDIYO

As I came down from Cundiyo,
Upon the road to Chimayo
    I met three women walking;
Each held a sorrow to her breast,
And one of them a small cross pressed —
    Three black-shawled women walking.

"Now why is it that you must go
Up the long road to Cundiyo?"
    The old one did the talking:
"I go to bless a dying son."
"And I a sweetheart never won."
    Three women slowly walking.

The third one opened wide her shawl
And showed a new-born baby small
    That slept without a sorrow:
"And I, in haste that we be wed —
Too late, too late, if he be dead!
    The Padre comes tomorrow."

As I went up to Cundiyo,
In the grey dawn from Chimayo,
    I met three women walking;
And over paths of sand and rocks
Were men who carried a long box —
    Beside three women walking.

ELIOT PORTER

Frozen Apples, New Mexico, 1966

Dry-transfer photograph

Museum of New Mexico, Museum of Fine Arts

Gift of Dale and Sylvia Bell, 1986. ©1990 Amon Carter
Museum, Fort Worth, Texas, Bequest of the artist.

MANZANITA

From the Spanish

Little red apple upon the tree,
If you are not in love, fall in love with me! . . .

From me this night you shall not go,
Not till the dawn, when the first cocks crow.

ANSEL ADAMS

Moonrise, Hernandez, New Mexico, 1941
Gelatin-silver photograph
Museum of New Mexico, Museum of Fine Arts
Gift of Museum of New Mexico Foundation, 1982

CHULA LA MAÑANA

From the Spanish

Pretty is the morning,
    Pretty is the day.
When the moon comes up
    It is light as day.

    Fortune's wheel keeps turning!

Yes, Fortune has its ups and downs,
    Fortune is a bubble.
It was all for a married woman
    I had my trouble.

    Fortune's wheel keeps turning!

It was eight o'clock at the bridge,
    And nine at Jesus Maria,
But before I could reach her door,
    I was caught by her fat old *tía!*

    Fortune's wheel keeps turning!

JOHN C. COLLIER JR.

Cordova, Rio Arriba County, NM (Sheep Belonging to Blas Chavez),
1943

Modern gelatin-silver photograph

Museum of New Mexico, Museum of Fine Arts

The Pinewood Foundation Collection, Farm Security Admin.
photographs, with additional support from Barbara Erdman,
Library of Congress, 1990

"CHRIST IS BORN IN BETHLEHEM"

A New Mexico Nursery Rhyme

Cristo nació is what the rooster said,
And the hen said, *En Belen!*
The goats were so curious that they said
Vamos a ver—let us go see!
But the wise old sheep said,
No es menester!—there's no need of it!

> *Cristo nacio*
> *En Belen!*
> *Vamos a ver*—
> *No es menester!*

EMIL BISTTRAM

Peace, 1930
Lithograph
Museum of New Mexico, Museum of Fine Arts
Bequest of Vivian Sloan Fiske, 1978

LA MUERTE DE LA VIEJA

There were four old women as old as she
Who knelt in the room where the sick one lay,
And the *resador* with his book of prayers
Who sat by her side all night to pray.

In the morning light her face was grey
As the ash that covered the embers still,
The black-shawled women had never stirred
And the old man's voice was hoarse and shrill.

The crucifix laid on her heaving breast
Moved with her harsh breath up and down,
And her mouth like a chicken's gaped for air
With a noise that the droning could not drown.

The sunlight poured through the open door
Where I stood and wondered how it could be
That the old, old woman with such great strength
Fought with the force we could not see.

As she had fought long years ago
Through child-bed pain, now her body thin
Strove to the last with the mid-wife Death,
Till silence ushered her new life in.

PAUL BURLIN

The Sacristan of Trampas, 1918
Oil on canvas
Museum of New Mexico, Museum of Fine Arts
Museum acquisition, 1922

JUAN QUINTANA

The goat-herd follows his flock
Over the sandy plain,
And the goats nibble the rabbit-bush
Acrid with desert rain.

Old Juan Quintana's coat
Is a faded purple blue,
And his hat is a warm plum-brown,
And his trousers a tawny hue;

He is sunburnt like the hills,
And his eyes have a strange goat-look,
And when I came on him alone,
He suddenly quivered and shook.

Out in the hills all day,
The trees do funny things—
And a horse shaped like a man
Rose up from the ground on wings.

And a burro came and stood
With a cross, and preached to the flock,
While old Quintana sat
As cold as ice on a rock.

And sometimes the mountains move,
And the mesa turns about,
And Juan Quintana thinks he's lost,
Till a neighbor hears him shout.

And they say with a little laugh
That he isn't quite right, up here;
And they'll have to get a *muchacho*
To help with the flock next year.

ELIAS RIVERA

Fiesta at Santa Fe, 1985
Oil on canvas
Museum of New Mexico, Museum of Fine Arts
Gift of Aviation Materials Management, Inc., 1987

PETROLINO'S COMPLAINT

The old ways have changed since you walked
      here,
    But worst of all is the way the people have
      become.
They have no hearts, and their minds are like
      putty,
    And if you ask for conversation, they might as
      well be dumb!

Though I am old, and my sight is not good,
    And I don't hear as well —*muy verdad*—as some,
With my stick I can walk faster than many,
    And my mind travels faster than a man's with
      no tongue!

The young have no thought for their elders,
    Their ranches are now no bigger than your
      thumb,
The young men work in the mines in Colora'o,
    Or they sit and warm their stomachs in the sun!

The girls spend their money on big hats and velvet,
    But when they would marry, they haven't the
      sum;
And the old songs and dances are forgotten,
    As the Saints will be forgotten —if they go on
      as they've begun!

I have gone looking through hillsides and canyons,
    Through all the *placitas* where we used to run;
But the old ways have changed since you walked
      here,
    And a goat is more sociable than a man that is
      dumb!

PAUL STRAND

Shop, le Bacares (Pyrenees-Orientals, France), 1950
Gold-toned, varnished gelatin-silver photograph
Museum of New Mexico, Museum of Fine Arts
Gift of Michael Hoffman, 1990

EL COYOTITO

From the Spanish

When I left Hermosillo
   My tears fell like rain,
But the little red flower
   Consoled my pain.

I am like the coyote
   That rolls them, and goes
Trotting off side-ways,
   And nobody knows.

The green pine has fallen,
   Where the doves used to pair;
Now the black one may find on returning
   Little tow-heads with sandy hair!

The adobe is gone
   Where my sword hung suspended;
Why worry—when everything's
   At the last ended?

The adobe is gone
   Where my mirror was bright,
And the small cedar tree
   Is the rabbit's tonight.

The cactus is bare
   Where the tunas were sweet;
No longer need you be jealous
   Of the women I meet.

Friends, if you see her
   In the hills up above,
Don't tell her that I am in prison—
   For she is my love.

NOTES ON POEMS

By Alice Corbin

Page 55. *Indian Songs:* Based on the literal translations made by Miss Frances Densmore. (Chippewa Music, Bulletins 45 and 53, Bureau of American Ethnology.) Indian poetry in its most characteristic form, is at the opposite pole from narrative or descriptive poetry, or even from the usual occidental lyric, which gives a double image, i.e., the original emotional stimulus *through* the thought or emotion aroused by it. Indian poetry is seldom self-conscious to this degree. It gives the naked image, or symbol, which is itself the emotional stimulus. The distinction is subtle, but one who would interpret or translate Indian verse must perceive it.

Page 61. *Corn-Grinding Song:* This song was given me by Canuto Suaza, a Tesuque Indian, who translated it for me from the Tewa, in both Spanish and English. My rendering is as direct as possible.

Page 63. *The Green Corn Dance:* The symbolism of Indian dances, carried out in every detail of costume, gesture, and song, takes such a hold upon the imagination that one becomes only half conscious of the dancers, lost in that archetypal world of which the dance furnishes a symbolic mirror.

Page 95. *Madre Maria:* From a Spanish version obtained by Miss Barbara Freire-Marreco from an Indian woman at the Santa Clara Pueblo. The Indians have preserved many of the traditional and popular Spanish New Mexico songs. This is an old song, probably brought to New Mexico by the early Franciscans, other versions of it having been found in South America. The final stanza is obviously a local addition.

Pages 99 and 103. *Manzanita* and the New Mexico nursery rhyme *Christ Is Born in Bethlehem* were given me by Mrs. N. Howard Thorp of Santa Fe.

Page 101. *Chula la Mañana* is a free translation of a popular New Mexico song. (The word *tía* means *aunt.*) There are many versions of this song in the Southwest and in Old Mexico.

Page 111. *El Coyotito* is from the Spanish version in Charles F. Lummis' *The Land of Poco Tiempo.* Mr. Lummis himself has made an excellent translation of the song, but has left out, perhaps judiciously, some of the tang. His translation, however, is fitted to the music accompanying the original song while mine has created a new rhythm.